Palermo Travel Guide 2024

"Architectural Marvels: Palermo's Stunning Palaces and Churches"

By

Logan M. William

Table of contents

Introduction

Welcome to Palermo, the vibrant capital city of Sicily, Italy. Nestled on the northern coast of the island, Palermo is a cultural melting pot with a rich tapestry of history, architecture, and cuisine. From its ancient Greek roots to its Arab and Norman influences, Palermo boasts a diverse heritage that is reflected in its architecture, cuisine, and way of life.

Palermo is characterized by its Mediterranean climate, with hot summers and mild winters, making it an ideal destination year-round. The city's layout is a blend of ancient and modern, with narrow cobblestone streets winding through historic neighborhoods and bustling boulevards lined with palm trees. Local transportation options include buses, trams, and taxis, providing convenient access to Palermo's many attractions.

Top Attractions in Palermo

Palermo is home to a wealth of cultural and historical landmarks, including the majestic

Norman Palace, the exquisite Cappella Palatina, and the imposing Cathedral of Palermo.

Visitors can explore the vibrant markets of Ballarò and Vucciria, wander through the lush gardens of Villa Giulia, or take in panoramic views of the city from the iconic Mount Pellegrino.

Cultural Experiences in Palermo

Immerse yourself in Palermo's rich cultural heritage by attending a traditional Sicilian puppet show, sampling local street food specialties like arancini and sfincione, or visiting the vibrant street art scene in the historic Kalsa district.

Art lovers can explore the collections of the Palazzo Abatellis and the Museo Archeologico Regionale, while music enthusiasts can enjoy live performances of traditional Sicilian folk music in local venues.

Dining and Culinary Delights

No visit to Palermo is complete without indulging in the city's renowned culinary delights. From savory street food to elegant seafood dishes, Palermo offers a diverse array of dining options to suit every palate. Sample traditional Sicilian dishes like pasta con le sarde, caponata, and cannoli, or savor fresh seafood at waterfront trattorias overlooking the Mediterranean Sea.

Outdoor Adventures and Natural Attractions

Escape the hustle and bustle of the city and explore Palermo's natural beauty. Hike through the rugged landscapes of Monte Pellegrino, swim in the crystal-clear waters of Mondello Beach, or take a boat tour of the stunning Zingaro Nature Reserve.

Outdoor enthusiasts can also explore the picturesque countryside of Sicily on a guided cycling tour or horseback riding excursion.

Nightlife and Entertainment

As the sun sets over Palermo, the city comes alive with a vibrant nightlife scene. From trendy rooftop bars to historic wine bars, Palermo offers a variety of venues for evening entertainment. Enjoy live music performances, dance the night away at a local nightclub, or simply stroll through the city's lively piazzas and soak up the atmosphere.

Shopping and Souvenirs

Discover unique treasures and souvenirs in Palermo's eclectic shops and markets. Browse handmade ceramics and pottery in the artisan workshops of the historic Vucciria Market, shop for stylish fashion and accessories in the trendy boutiques of Via Roma, or sample local wines and delicacies at the bustling Mercato del Capo.

Accommodations

From boutique hotels in historic palazzos to charming bed and breakfasts in the city center, Palermo offers a range of accommodations to suit every taste and budget. Stay in the heart of the action near the Quattro Canti, or retreat to a peaceful oasis in the countryside surrounding the city.

Day Trips from Palermo

Venture beyond the city limits and discover the beauty of Sicily on a day trip from Palermo. Visit the ancient Greek ruins of Segesta and Selinunte, explore the historic town of Cefalù with its stunning Norman cathedral, or take a scenic drive along the coast to the picturesque Castellammare del Golfo fishing village

In conclusion, Palermo is a captivating destination that offers something for everyone. Whether you're drawn to its rich history and culture, its delicious cuisine, or its stunning natural beauty, Palermo promises an unforgettable experience that will leave you longing to return again and again

Chapter One

Welcome to Palermo

Step into a city where ancient history coexists with the vibrant pulse of contemporary life. Palermo extends a warm embrace to visitors, inviting them to wander through its labyrinthine streets, soak in the dynamic markets, and savor the flavors of Sicilian cuisine.

The historic center whispers stories of empires, conquests, and the enduring spirit of its people, offering a captivating journey through time. Palermo's roots delve deep into antiquity, echoing the tales of Phoenician and Carthaginian settlements.

 Over the centuries, the city has been shaped by Roman, Byzantine, Arab, and Norman influences, each leaving an indelible mark on its architecture, culture, and traditions.

Overview of Palermo's Culture

Palermo's culture is a mosaic of influences, reflecting the city's strategic location at the crossroads of the Mediterranean. From the intricate mosaics of Monreale to the Moorish architecture of the Palazzo dei Normanni, the city's cultural heritage is a testament to its diverse past.

The arts, music, and religious celebrations further showcase the fusion of traditions, creating a dynamic and unique cultural identity distinctly Palermitan.

Cultural Kaleidoscope

Palermo's culture is a vibrant kaleidoscope, blending diverse influences into a harmonious whole.

Architectural masterpieces like the Palazzo dei Normanni and the awe-inspiring Cathedral of Monreale showcase the city's artistic prowess.

Yet, Palermo's culture isn't confined to stone and mortar; it resonates in the music that fills the Air during local festivals, the art that graces its galleries, and the flavors that define Sicilian cuisine. The city's cultural identity celebrates its unique position as a crossroads of civilizations.

Chapter Two

Getting There

With its allure on the northern coast of Sicily, Palermo is well-connected and accessible for travelers seeking to explore its rich cultural tapestry. Getting to Palermo is a seamless journey with various transportation options catering to different preferences and needs.

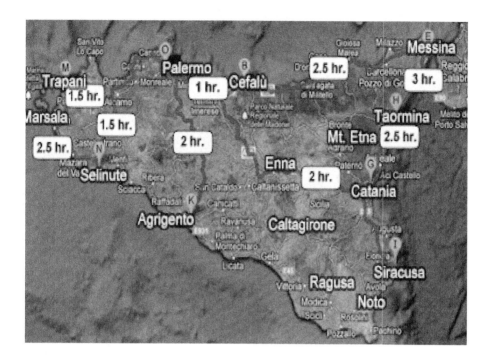

Transportation

By Air
Palermo is served by Falcone-Borsellino Airport, also known as Punta Raisi Airport. It serves as the main entry point for both domestic and international planes. Major airlines operate regular flights connecting Palermo to key cities across Europe and Italy.

By Sea

For those seeking a scenic approach, ferries and hydrofoils operate from various Italian cities, including Naples and Genoa, providing an alternative mode of transport. The ferry terminal is conveniently located.

By Train

An extensive rail network connects Palermo to major cities within Sicily and mainland Italy. The train journey through the picturesque landscapes adds a touch of charm to your arrival.

By Car

 Rental cars are readily available at the airport and city center for a flexible and adventurous option. The well-maintained road network allows visitors to explore at their own pace.

Arrival at Falcone-Borsellino Airport

Punta Raisi Airport, sometimes called Falcone-Borsellino Airport.

Situated approximately 35 kilometers west of Palermo, the airport is a modern facility equipped with services and amenities to ensure a smooth arrival.Ground transportation options from the airport include taxis, rental cars, and shuttle services. Taxis are readily available outside the arrivals area, providing a convenient transfer to the city.

Public Transportation in Palermo

Bus Services

Palermo boasts an efficient and extensive bus network operated by AMAT. Buses connect key points within the city and its outskirts, offering an affordable and convenient way to explore.

Trams and Metro

The city features a tram system and a metro line, providing additional options for efficient and quick transportation within Palermo.

Walking and Bicycles

Given the compact size of the city center, walking is a delightful way to explore Palermo's historic streets. Additionally, bicycle rentals are available for those wanting a more active exploration.

Navigating Palermo is a seamless experience with diverse transportation options catering to every traveler's preference. Whether arriving by Air, Sea, or land, and traversing the city by public transport or on foot, each mode of transportation adds to the unique charm of discovering Palermo's treasures.

Chapter Three

Where to Stay

With its rich history and vibrant culture, Palermo offers diverse accommodation options to suit every traveler's preferences.

From luxurious hotels showcasing Sicilian elegance to charming boutique stays immersed in the city's historic charm, choosing where to stay in Palermo is integral to crafting an immersive and enjoyable experience.

Luxury Hotels

Palermo boasts an array of upscale hotels that offer a blend of sophistication and comfort. These establishments often feature lavish amenities, spa services, and exquisite dining options.

Boutique Hotels

For those seeking a more intimate and unique experience, boutique hotels throughout the city provide personalized service and distinctive decor, often reflecting Palermo's cultural influences.

Budget-Friendly Options

Budget-conscious travelers can find an assortment of guesthouses, hostels, and affordable hotels, providing comfort without breaking the bank. These options are often situated in central locations, making them convenient for exploring the city.

Apartments and Vacation Rentals

Experience Palermo like a local by opting for apartments or vacation rentals. This choice offers a sense of independence and the opportunity to immerse yourself in the city's daily life.

Recommended Neighborhoods

La Kalsa

This historic neighborhood is known for its narrow streets, vibrant markets, and proximity to key attractions like the Palermo Cathedral and the Ballarò Market. Accommodations here offer a charming blend of authenticity and accessibility.

Albergheria

As one of Palermo's oldest districts, Albergheria is a captivating area with historic sites, including the Palazzo dei Normanni and the famous Quattro Canti. Staying here provides a central location for exploring the city's cultural treasures.

Castellammare

Overlooking the Sea, Castellammare offers a picturesque setting with views of the Gulf of Palermo. The neighborhood features a mix of historic and modern elements, making it an ideal choice for those seeking a coastal retreat.

Vucciria

If you're drawn to Palermo's vibrant nightlife, the Vucciria district is a lively choice. Known for its street food, markets, and eclectic atmosphere, accommodations here place you in the midst of the city's dynamic energy.

The right neighborhood and accommodation in Palermo are key to curating a memorable stay. Whether you prefer the historic charm of La Kalsa, the central allure of Albergheria, the coastal ambiance of Castellammare, or the lively atmosphere of Vucciria, each option contributes to the unique tapestry of your Palermo experience.

Chapter Four

Exploring the City

Palermo's charm lies in its ability to seamlessly blend ancient history with the vibrant pulse of contemporary life. As you explore the city, each step unveils a tapestry woven with tales of empires, artistic prowess, and the daily rhythms of Palermo's diverse neighborhoods.

Norman Palace and Palatine Chapel

Immerse yourself in the rich history of Palermo by visiting the Norman Palace. Explore its opulent rooms and be captivated by the mosaics in the Palatine Chapel, showcasing the city's multicultural influences.

Artistic Treasures

Palermo's museums, theaters, and festivals showcase a rich tapestry of arts and culture. Whether admiring Byzantine mosaics in the Palatine Chapel or attending a performance at Teatro Massimo, you are surrounded by the creativity and passion that define the city.

Cathedral of Palermo

A short stroll brings you to the Cathedral of Palermo, a grand structure that fuses Norman, Arab, and Gothic architectural elements. Marvel at the impressive exterior and discover its treasures, including royal tombs and sacred relics.

Ballarò Market

Dive into the lively street life of Palermo by exploring the Ballarò Market. This bustling marketplace offers a sensory feast with stalls brimming with fresh produce, local delicacies, and the vibrant energy of vendors haggling with customers.

Quattro Canti and Via Maqueda

Begin exploring the city's heart at Quattro Canti, a Baroque masterpiece where Via Maqueda and Via Vittorio Emanuele intersect. Flanked by elegant buildings, these streets lead you into the bustling heart of Palermo's historic center.

Palazzo dei Normanni

Explore the Palazzo dei Normanni, the Norman Palace, which symbolizes Palermo's historical significance. Take advantage of the impressive Palatine Chapel adorned with intricate mosaics.

Teatro Massimo

Revel in the grandeur of Teatro Massimo, one of Europe's largest opera houses. Admire its neoclassical architecture and consider catching a performance to experience the cultural heartbeat of Palermo.

Fontana Pretoria

Wander to Piazza Pretoria and discover the Fontana Pretoria, a magnificent fountain surrounded by sculptures. This Renaissance masterpiece adds a touch of elegance to the city's urban landscape.

Historical Marvels

Palermo's historic center, adorned with architectural masterpieces like the Norman Palace and the Palatine Chapel, is a testament to the city's multifaceted past.

 Each cobblestone street whispers tales of Phoenician, Arab, and Norman influences that have shaped its identity.

Coastal Allure

 The coastline beckons with golden beaches like Mondello and the picturesque charm of coastal towns like Cefalù. Palermo's proximity to the Sea adds a layer of tranquility, inviting you to unwind along the shores of the Mediterranean.

Markets and Street Life

Vucciria Market
Immerse yourself in the lively atmosphere of Vucciria Market, where the narrow streets come alive with vendors selling fresh produce, seafood, and Sicilian street food. It's a sensory journey through Palermo's culinary delights.

Capo Market
Capo Market invites you to explore its colorful stalls, offering everything from spices and olives to handmade crafts. The market provides an authentic glimpse into daily life in Palermo.

Street Art in Ballarò
Wander through the Ballarò district to discover vibrant street art adorning walls and buildings. This open-air gallery reflects Palermo's dynamic and contemporary cultural scene.

As you navigate Palermo's historic center, marvel at its architectural treasures, immerse yourself in the energy of its markets and embrace the fusion of past and present that defines this captivating city. Palermo's streets, monuments, and markets are an invitation to explore, discover, and savor the essence of Sicilian life.

Chapter Five

Culinary Delights

Palermo's culinary scene is a symphony of flavors, where the essence of Sicilian cuisine unfolds in a tapestry of tastes that reflect the island's rich history and diverse influences.

 From the tantalizing aroma of street food to the elegant dishes served in renowned restaurants, Palermo invites you to embark on a gastronomic journey.

The scent of Sicilian olive oil and the flavors of fresh seafood delicacies linger in the Air. From the vibrant markets of Ballarò to the traditional trattorias, Palermo's culinary scene captivates your senses, inviting you to savor the essence of Sicilian cuisine.

Local Sicilian Cuisine:

Seafood Extravaganza

Given Palermo's coastal location, seafood features prominently in local cuisine.

From the iconic Sicilian seafood pasta to fresh catches grilled with Sicilian herbs, every dish pays homage to the bounty of the Mediterranean.

Arancini

Savor the iconic arancini, deep-fried rice balls filled with ragù (meat sauce), mozzarella, and peas. These golden orbs are not just a snack but a culinary delight that encapsulates Sicilian comfort food.

Caponata

Delight in caponata, a savory-sweet eggplant dish that combines tomatoes, olives, capers, and celery flavors. This traditional Sicilian antipasto offers a taste of the island's agricultural abundance.

Sicilian Olive Oil and Citrus Fruits

Begin your culinary exploration with the foundation of Sicilian cuisine—extra virgin olive oil. Renowned for its quality, Sicilian olive oil enhances various dishes. Citrus fruits, like blood oranges and lemons, add a refreshing twist to savory and sweet creations.

Must-Try Dishes and Street Food

Sfincione

Indulge in sfincione, a thick Sicilian pizza topped with tomatoes, onions, breadcrumbs, and olive oil. Often enjoyed as a street food snack, sfincione showcases the simplicity and depth of Sicilian flavors.

Cannoli

Treat yourself to cannoli, a quintessential Sicilian dessert. These crispy pastry tubes filled with sweet ricotta and adorned with pistachios or chocolate chips are a delightful ending to any meal.

Panelle e Crocchè

Explore the world of Sicilian street food with panelles, chickpea fritters, crocchè, and potato croquettes. These savory bites are commonly enjoyed as snacks, offering a quick taste of local flavors on the go.

Popular Cafés and Restaurants

Antica Focacceria San Francesco

Step into history at Antica Focacceria San Francesco, a historic eatery from 1834. Known for its traditional Sicilian dishes, it's a culinary journey through time.

Trattoria Da Pino

Experience the warmth of Trattoria Da Pino, a family-run restaurant serving classic Sicilian fare. From pasta dishes to seafood specialities, the menu reflects the essence of local cuisine.

Bar Touring

For a quintessential Palermo experience, visit Bar Touring. This historic café offers traditional Sicilian pastries and granita, a refreshing frozen dessert.

Palermo's culinary scene celebrates tradition, innovation, and the island's bountiful resources. Whether indulging in seafood by the Sea, savoring street food in bustling markets, or dining in historic establishments, each culinary experience in Palermo is a testament to Sicily's gastronomic richness.

Chapter Six

Day Trips and Excursions

Palermo's charm extends beyond city limits, offering enchanting day trips and excursions that unveil the surrounding areas' diverse landscapes and cultural treasures. From historic gems to pristine coastal retreats, these excursions promise a delightful exploration of Sicily's wonders.

Excursions to Monreale and Cefalù

- **Monreale**

Embark on a journey to Monreale, just a short drive from Palermo. Visit the stunning Cathedral of Monreale, a UNESCO World Heritage site renowned for its breathtaking mosaics depicting biblical narratives. Explore the tranquil cloister adorned with intricate columns and arches.

- **Cefalù**

Discover the coastal charm of Cefalù, a picturesque town framed by a dramatic rocky headland. Visit the magnificent Cefalù Cathedral, an iconic example of Norman architecture. Stroll through the charming streets, relax on the sandy beaches, and soak in the laid-back atmosphere of this coastal gem.

Beaches and Coastal Getaways

- **Mondello Beach**

Escape to Mondello Beach, a beloved retreat just a short drive from Palermo. With its crystalline waters and soft golden sands, Mondello offers an idyllic setting for sunbathing, swimming, and indulging in delicious seafood at beachfront trattorias.

- **San Vito Lo Capo**

Venture to San Vito Lo Capo, known for its pristine beaches and turquoise waters. This coastal town offers a relaxing escape, and the striking views of the Riserva dello Zingaro make it an ideal destination for nature enthusiasts.

Nature Reserves and Hiking Options

- **Riserva dello Zingaro**

Immerse yourself in the natural beauty of Riserva dello Zingaro, Sicily's first nature reserve. Hike along scenic trails that lead to secluded coves, enjoy panoramic views of the Mediterranean, and encounter diverse flora and fauna in this protected coastal area.

- **Madonie Regional Natural Park**

Explore the Madonie Regional Natural Park, a haven for hiking enthusiasts. With its rugged landscapes, charming mountain villages, and well-marked trails, this park offers a variety of routes suitable for all levels of hikers.

- **Monte Pellegrino**

Conquer Monte Pellegrino, the iconic mountain overlooking Palermo. Hike to the summit for panoramic views of the city and the Gulf of Palermo.

The Sanctuary of Santa Rosalia, perched on the mountain, adds a spiritual touch to the hiking experience.

These day trips and excursions from Palermo unveil the diverse facets of Sicily, from historical treasures to coastal paradises and pristine nature reserves. Each destination invites exploration, promising a rewarding escape into the beauty that surrounds this captivating region.

Chapter Seven

Arts and Culture

Palermo's rich arts and cultural scene weaves a tapestry of history, architecture, and contemporary expressions. From world-class museums to lively theatres and vibrant festivals, Palermo invites you to explore the depth of its artistic heritage and immerse yourself in cultural experiences.

Museums and Art Galleries

- **Palazzo Abatellis** - Regional Gallery of Sicily

Discover Palermo's artistic treasures at Palazzo Abatellis, a Gothic palace housing the Regional Gallery of Sicily. Marvel at Renaissance and Baroque masterpieces, including works by Antonello da Messina and Giuseppe Patania.

- **Palazzo dei Normanni** - Royal Palace

Visit the Palazzo dei Normanni, where the Royal Palace hosts the Palatine Chapel and its stunning Byzantine mosaics. Explore the palace's various rooms and galleries, each echoing with the whispers of Sicily's history.

- **Galleria d'Arte Moderna (GAM)**

Immerse yourself in contemporary art at the Galleria d'Arte Moderna, showcasing works by Italian and Sicilian artists from the 19th to the 21st century. The museum offers a glimpse into the evolution of Sicilian art.

Palermo's Theatres and Performance Arts

- **Teatro Massimo**

Step into the grandeur of Teatro Massimo, one of Europe's largest opera houses. Attend a performance to experience the cultural heartbeat of Palermo, whether it's a classical opera or a modern production.

- **Teatro Politeama**

Explore Teatro Politeama, a majestic theater hosting various performances, including ballets, concerts, and theatrical productions. The neoclassical architecture and vibrant cultural calendar make it a centrepiece of Palermo's artistic life.

Traditional Festivals and Events

- **Festa di Santa Rosalia**

  Join the vibrant celebrations of Festa di Santa Rosalia, Palermo's patron saint. Held in July, this festival features processions, fireworks, and a lively atmosphere throughout the city, culminating in a grand procession to Monte Pellegrino.

- **Festival di Morgana**

Dive into the world of contemporary arts at the Festival di Morgana. This annual event showcases diverse performances, from theater and dance to music and multimedia installations, attracting artists and art enthusiasts alike.

- **Carnival of Acireale**

Experience the lively Carnival of Acireale, located a short distance from Palermo. This vibrant celebration features colorful parades, elaborate costumes, and traditional music, adding a touch of joy to the winter months.

Palermo's arts and culture scene encapsulates the essence of Sicily's history, creativity, and passion. Whether exploring timeless masterpieces in museums, attending a performance in one of the grand theatres, or participating in the lively energy of traditional festivals, each cultural experience in Palermo is an invitation to connect with the city's soul.

Chapter Eight

Shopping in Palermo

Palermo's vibrant streets and bustling markets offer a shopping experience that reflects the city's eclectic culture and rich history. From local markets brimming with fresh produce to artisan shops showcasing unique handcrafts, shopping in Palermo is a journey of discovery and a celebration of Sicilian craftsmanship.

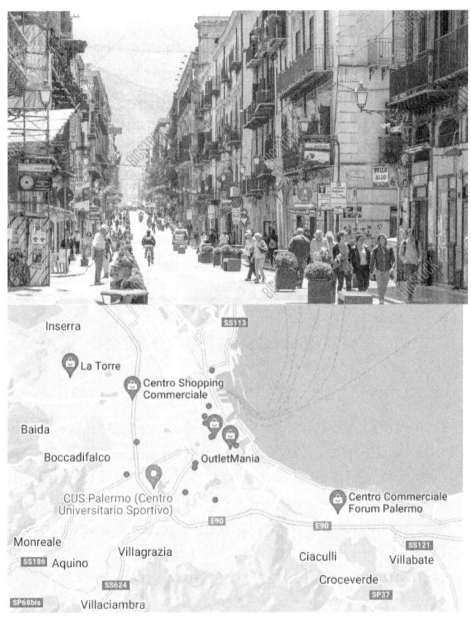

Local Markets and Bazaars

- **Ballarò Market**

Immerse yourself in the lively atmosphere of Ballarò Market, one of Palermo's oldest and most iconic markets. Located in the historic Albergheria district, Ballarò is a sensory feast, with stalls teeming with fresh produce, spices, seafood, and local street food. Engage with vendors, sample Sicilian delicacies, and experience the vibrant street life.

- **Capo Market**

Wander through the narrow lanes of Capo Market, where colorful stalls showcase an array of fruits, vegetables, meats, and local specialities. This market, nestled between Palermo's historic streets, offers an authentic glimpse into daily Sicilian life. Please take advantage of the opportunity to explore the adjacent Vucciria Market, known for its lively ambience and diverse offerings.

- **Vucciria Market**

Once a bustling fish market, Vucciria has transformed into a dynamic market with a diverse range of products. From fresh produce to clothing and handicrafts, Vucciria's stalls present a mix of traditional and contemporary offerings. This market is not just a shopping destination; it's a cultural experience.

Unique Souvenirs and Handicrafts

- **Sicilian Ceramics**

Explore the world of Sicilian ceramics, renowned for its vibrant colors and intricate designs. Hand-painted plates, tiles, and decorative items featuring traditional motifs make unique and authentic souvenirs. Visit artisan shops or markets like La Kalsa to discover these timeless pieces.

- **Handwoven Textiles**

Palermo's markets and boutique shops showcase exquisite handwoven textiles, including intricate lacework and vibrant fabrics. Look for handmade linens, shawls, and scarves adorned with traditional Sicilian patterns, providing a touch of local craftsmanship.

- **Sicilian Marzipan**

Indulge in the sweet delights of Sicilian marzipan. Shaped into intricate figures and fruits, marzipan creations are delicious and make for charming and edible souvenirs. Seek out patisseries or pastry shops to find these delightful treats.

Traditional Sicilian Puppets

Palermo is famous for its traditional Sicilian puppets, known as "pups." These elaborately crafted marionettes depict characters from Sicilian folklore and historical tales. Artisan workshops and souvenir shops offer these unique and culturally rich keepsakes.

Shopping in Palermo extends beyond acquiring goods; it's an opportunity to immerse yourself in the city's vibrant culture, connect with local artisans, and bring home treasures that tell the story of Sicily's craftsmanship and traditions.

Chapter Nine
Practical Tips

Weather

Palermo enjoys a Mediterranean climate characterized by hot, dry summers and mild, wet winters. Summers (June to September) are ideal for beachgoers, while spring (April to May) and fall (October to November) offer pleasant temperatures for exploring the city and surrounding areas.

Best Time to Visit

Spring and fall shoulder seasons are often considered the best times to visit Palermo. The weather is comfortable, and attractions are less crowded. If you prefer a lively atmosphere and warm beach days, summer is the peak tourist season.

Local Etiquette and Customs

Cultural Sensitivity
Sicilians are known for their warm hospitality, so reciprocating kindness is appreciated. When entering someone's home, it's customary to bring a small gift as a token of appreciation.

Dress Modestly in Churches
When visiting churches and religious sites, dress modestly. Cover your shoulders and avoid wearing shorts. This demonstrates respect for local customs and religious traditions.

Greeting Customs
Traditional Italian greetings involve a kiss on both cheeks. However, in more formal settings, a handshake is appropriate. Use titles like "Signore" (Mr.) and "Signora" (Mrs.) when addressing people you don't know well.

Safety Guidelines

General Safety

Palermo is generally a safe city, but like any urban destination, it's wise to be cautious in crowded areas. Keep an eye on your belongings, especially in busy markets and tourist attractions.

Public Transportation Safety

Palermo's public transportation is generally safe, but be vigilant against pickpocketing, especially in crowded buses or trains. When taking public transit, be sure your tickets are valid at all times.

Emergency Numbers

Know the local emergency numbers. In Italy, the general emergency number is 112. For medical emergencies, call 118, and for the police, call 113.

Health Precautions

Carry necessary medications and health supplies. Make sure your travel insurance includes emergency medical coverage. Make sure your travel insurance includes emergency medical coverage. Be aware of food hygiene and sip water from bottles or treated sources.

With its captivating blend of history, culture, and coastal beauty, Palermo invites visitors to immerse themselves in the unique tapestry of Sicilian life. By considering practical tips related to weather, local etiquette, and safety, you can enhance your experience and fully appreciate Palermo's warmth and charm.

 Whether strolling through historic streets, indulging in local cuisine, or enjoying the Mediterranean sun, Palermo promises a memorable and enriching journey.

Conclusion

As travelers conclude their journey through the vibrant streets of Palermo, they depart with hearts full of memories and a deeper appreciation for the city's rich history, cultural diversity, and culinary delights.

Palermo, the capital of Sicily, captivates with its blend of ancient ruins, Baroque architecture, bustling markets, and seaside promenades, offering a tapestry of experiences that leave a lasting impression on all who wander its cobblestone streets and bask in its Mediterranean ambiance.

In concluding their visit to Palermo, travelers are encouraged to reflect on the highlights of their journey and savor the moments that made their time in the city truly unforgettable.

Whether it was exploring the grandeur of the Norman Palace, indulging in Sicilian street food at the lively Ballarò Market, or admiring the intricate mosaics of the Cappella Palatina, each experience was a testament to Palermo's enduring allure and cultural richness.

As travelers bid farewell to Palermo, they are offered a few final recommendations to ensure their memories of the city remain vivid and cherished:

1. Capture the Essence: Take time to capture the essence of Palermo through photographs, sketches, or journal entries, preserving the beauty and authenticity of the city's sights, sounds, and flavors.

2. Immerse Yourself: Dive deeper into Palermo's culture and traditions by attending a local festival, participating in a cooking class, or striking up a conversation with a friendly local to gain insight into the city's vibrant way of life.

3. Savor the Flavors: Indulge in the culinary delights of Sicily by sampling traditional dishes like arancini, panelle, and cannoli at local trattorias, osterias, and street food stalls scattered throughout the city.

4. Embrace the Magic: Allow yourself to be enchanted by the magic of Palermo, whether it's by wandering through the historic alleyways of the Vucciria Market, watching the sunset over the Gulf of Palermo, or simply taking a moment to soak in the city's timeless beauty.

In the end, Palermo is more than just a destination—it's a mosaic of history, culture, and gastronomy that captivates the senses and leaves a lasting impression on all who visit. Whether you return to Palermo again or simply carry its spirit with you in your memories, may the magic of the city continue to inspire and enrich your travels for years to come. Arrivederci, Palermo, until we meet again.

Printed in Great Britain
by Amazon

40432999R00040